Electricity

Claire Llewellyn

Photography by Ray Moller

SEA-TO-SEA

Mankato Collingwood London

This edition first published in 2005 by
Sea-to-Sea Publications
1980 Lookout Drive
North Mankato
Minnesota 56003

ISBN 1-932889-35-3

Printed in China

Library of Congress Control Number: 2004103735

2 4 6 8 9 7 5 3

Published by arrangement with the Watts Publishing Group Ltd, London

Series advisor: Gill Matthews, nonfiction literacy consultant and Inset trainer
Editor: Rachel Cooke
Series design: Peter Scoulding
Designer: James Marks
Photography: Ray Moller unless otherwise credited

Acknowledgements: Peter Frischmuth/Still Pictures: front cover, 6.Glen Dimplex UK Ltd: 9t. Nick
Hawkes/Ecoscene: 21b. Tony Page/Ecoscene: 13t, 23tl. Paul Thompson/Ecoscene: 12b.
Thanks to our models: Chloe Chetty, Nicole Davies, Georgia Farrell, Alex Green,
Madison Hanley, Aaron Hibbert, Chetan Johal, Henry Moller, Kane Yoon.

Contents

We use electricity

Every day we use electricity,

when we turn on a light...

a computer...

Make a list
or draw
pictures of
three ways in
which you use
electricity.

or a
cassette
player.

Electric light

Electricity gives us many things.
It gives us light.

▲ *Electric lights help us see in the dark.*

Switch on a flashlight and look at it. What part of it gives out light?

 *Headlight*

Lamp

Flashlight

Electric heat

Electricity gives us heat. It heats our homes, food, and water.

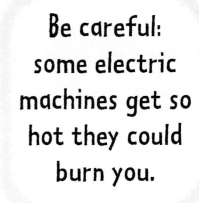

▶ *Electricity makes us hot drinks.*

Be careful: some electric machines get so hot they could burn you.

8

Electricity heats a room.

Electricity cooks bread in a toaster.

Electric machines

Many machines run on electricity. They help us do lots of things.

► *This machine washes the clothes.*

We plug many machines into a socket. This gives them the electricity they need to work.

◄ *This machine cleans the carpet.*

► *This machine dries our hair.*

11

Making electricity

Electricity is made in power stations. It flows into our homes.

Electricity flows from power stations...

along metal wires...

Never touch
any part of your
home's electricity.
It is very
dangerous.

*and into
our homes.*

Batteries

Batteries store electricity. Machines that run on batteries are easy to carry around.

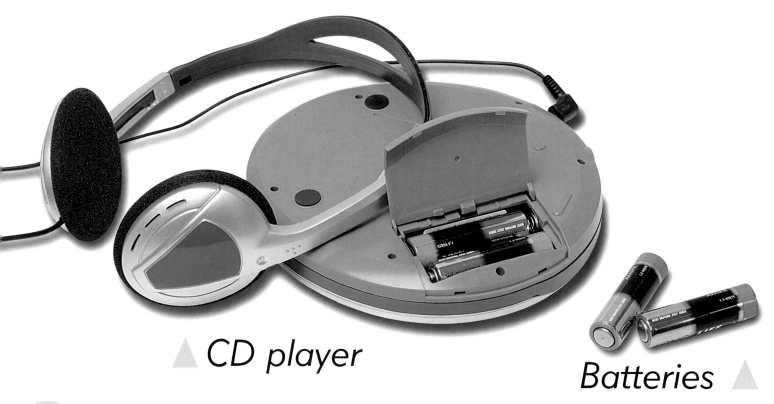

▲ *CD player*

Batteries ▲

▼ Radio

Batteries don't last forever. Which of these flashlights needs new ones?

▼ Hand-held computer game

Electric switches

Electricity flows into machines when we switch them on.

On

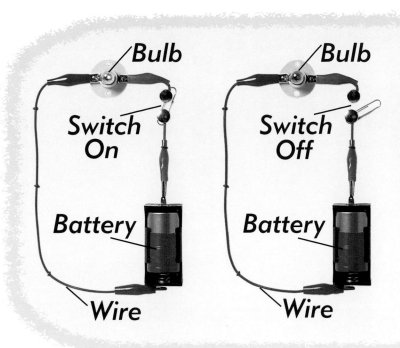

Bulb

Bulb

Switch On

Switch Off

Battery

Battery

Wire

Wire

Electricity flows around in a loop called a circuit. When you turn a switch off, you break the circuit, so the electricity stops flowing and the bulb goes out.

It stops flowing when we switch machines off.

◄ Off ►

The parts of a lamp

Different parts of electric machines have their own special names.

These are the electric parts of a lamp.

Socket ▽

Plug ▷

Cord ▲

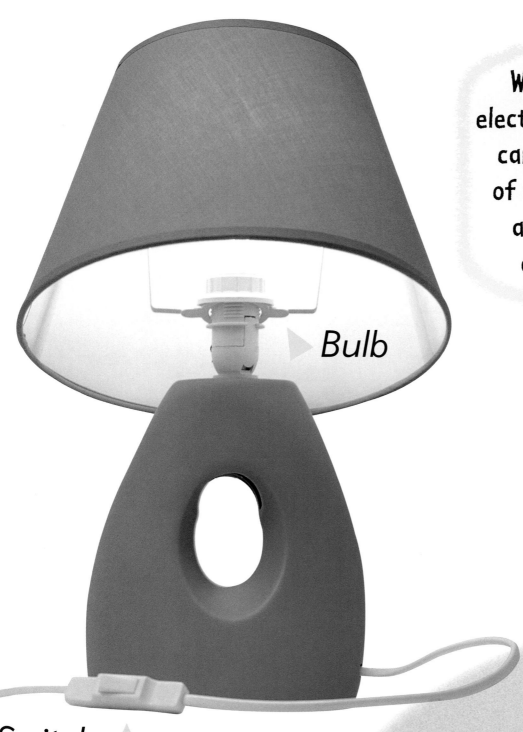

What other electric machines can you think of with a plug, a cord, and a switch?

Bulb

Switch

19

Electricity is dangerous

Electricity helps us but it can also hurt us. A strong flow of electricity can even kill us.

▶ *Do not play with plugs, sockets, or wires. They are dangerous.*

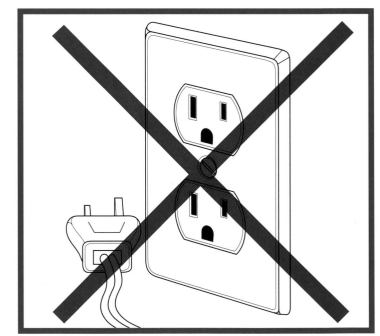

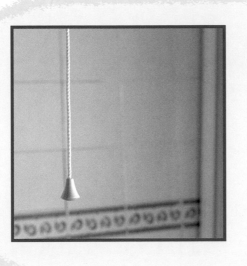

Electricity and water are dangerous together. In some countries, a pull cord in the bathroom keeps wet hands away from electric switches.

◀ *Do not play near electricity outside.*

I know that...

1 We use electricity.

2 Electricity gives light and heat.

3 Many machines run on electricity.

4 Electricity is made in power stations.

5 Electricity flows along wires to our homes.

6 Electricity is stored inside batteries.

7 A switch turns electric machines on and off.

8 Electric machines have parts with special names.

 ◀ *Switch*

9 Electricity is dangerous and can kill.

10 I must never play with electricity.

Index

batteries 14, 15, 23
bulb 17, 19
circuit 17
computer 5, 15
cord 18, 19
heat 8, 9, 22
lamp 7, 18, 19

light 4, 6, 7, 22
machines 8, 10, 11, 16, 17, 18, 19, 22, 23
plug 11, 18, 19, 20, 23
power stations 12, 22
radio 15

socket 18, 20
switch 7, 16, 17, 19, 21, 23
Walkman 14
wires 13, 20, 23

About this book

I Know That! is designed to introduce children to the process of gathering information and using reference books, one of the key skills needed to begin more formal learning at school. For this reason, each book's structure reflects the information books children will use later in their learning career—with key information in the main text and additional facts and ideas in the captions. The panels give an opportunity for further activities, ideas, or discussions. The contents page and index are helpful reference guides.

The language is carefully chosen to be accessible to children just beginning to read. Illustrations support the text but also give information in their own right; active consideration and discussion of images is another key referencing skill. The main aim of the series is to build confidence—showing children how much they already know and giving them the ability to gather new information for themselves. With this in mind, the *I know that...* section at the end of the book is a simple way for children to revisit what they already know as well as what they have learned from reading the book.